GETTING THE MAIN IDEA

ALVIN KRAVITZ, Ed.D.
C. W. Post College

DAN DRAMER

MCP SKILLBOOSTER F

Y0-BLW-119

THE MCP SKILL-BY-SKILL PROGRAM CONTAINS WORKBOOKS
IN THE FOLLOWING READING-SKILL AREAS:

Building Word Power, B-F
Working With Facts and Details, C-F
Getting the Main Idea, B-F
Increasing Comprehension, B-F
Organizing Information, B-F
Using References, C-F
Following Directions, B-D

Copyright © 1983 by MODERN CURRICULUM PRESS, INC.
13900 Prospect Road, Cleveland, Ohio 44136

All rights reserved. Printed in the United States of America.
This book or parts thereof may not be reproduced in any form or mechanically
stored in any retrieval system without written permission from the publisher.
Published simultaneously in Canada by Globe/Modern Curriculum Press, Toronto.

ISBN 0-8136-1231-4   5 6 7 8 9 10   88 87 86

TABLE OF CONTENTS

GETTING THE MOST FROM YOUR SKILLBOOSTER	3
LADY LIBERTY	5
ELEPHANTS AT WORK	6
YELLOW HAIR	8
THE CAMELS ARE COMING!	10
TIME CAPSULES	12
KEYBOARD GENIUS	14
A GIANT FAKE	16
YANKEE DOODLE	18
A THREE-HUNDRED-YEAR-OLD SECRET	20
DISCOVERERS OF THE NORTH POLE	22
WHEN BIGGER IS BETTER	24
PIGEON POWER	26
THE HIGHWAYMAN WAS A WOMAN	28
LIFE FROM LIFE	30
A PROBLEM WITH ICE	32
AN AMERICAN SUCCESS STORY	34
WHY SAVE THE WHALES?	36
FIRST LADY OF THE SKY	38
A STRANGE ZOO	40
UNFINISHED STORIES	42
YOU WRITE THE ENDING	44
WHAT SHOULD BE DONE?	46
ANSWER KEY	47
SKILLS INDEX	Inside Back Cover

GETTING THE MOST FROM YOUR SKILLBOOSTER

CAN YOU FIND THE MAIN IDEA?

Think about the last book you read or the last movie or television show you watched. If somebody asked you to tell the story in one sentence, could you do it? Here is one sentence about a famous story: A girl falls down a rabbit hole and has many strange adventures in which she meets unusual creatures. That sentence tells the main idea of *Alice in Wonderland*. The main idea is the most important idea of a story, article, or even a paragraph.

MAIN IDEAS HELP YOU IN MANY WAYS

Main ideas are important. If you can understand the main ideas of what you read, hear, and watch, you understand the most important messages that are coming to you. You can also understand the most important things you learn at school. In addition, knowing the main ideas will help you listen to others and speak to them with understanding.

RECOGNIZING MAIN IDEAS IS A SKILL YOU CAN LEARN

This book is designed to help you learn different ways to recognize main ideas. You will learn to look for signals that show main ideas are coming. You will learn to find details that work together to support a main idea. You will learn to use outlines to find main ideas. This Skillbooster, *Getting the Main Idea,* will help you develop the skills you need to recognize main ideas.

RELAX AND ENJOY YOURSELF

The pages in this Skillbooster contain articles and stories on a great many topics. There are stories about people and events that are new to you. There are also stories about some familiar things. Relax as you read. Enjoy yourself. Remember that these are practice exercises, not tests.

LEARN FROM ANY MISTAKES

Read carefully and follow the directions. When you answer the questions, do your best. If your teacher permits you to check your own answers, look and see whether your answers are correct. If they are not, look back over the directions and the story. Then try to figure out why you made a mistake. Learn from your mistakes. That way, you are less likely to make the same kind of mistake the next time.

BECOME A BETTER READER

Now is the time for you to become a better reader by learning to recognize the main ideas. Don't forget to relax and enjoy yourself as you improve your skill.

Project Supervision: Dimensions & Directions, Ltd.
Cover Design: William E. Frost
Photo Research: Helena Frost
Editor: Eden Eskin

Photo Credits: Cover, Dimensions & Directions, Ltd.; 5, Port Authority of N.Y. & N.J.; 7, U.P.I.; 8, Library of Congress; 11, U.N.; 12, U.P.I.; 15, Dimensions & Directions, Ltd.; 17, N.Y. State Historical Assoc.; 19, Library of Congress; 21, R.K. Reddy Collection; 23, left and right, Culver Pictures, Inc.; center, Library of Congress; 25, St. Louis Regional Commerce & Growth Assoc.; 26, 27, 29, 30, Culver Pictures, Inc.; 32, 35, U.P.I.; 36, Animal Welfare Institute; 39, U.P.I.; 40, 41, Culver Pictures, Inc.; 42, U.N.; 43, U.P.I.; 44, British Tourist Authority; 46, Donald Monaco.

LADY LIBERTY

Dates are important in understanding some reading selections. Using a time line helps you follow the order in which events take place.

> Read the selection. Write the dates on which the events happened on the blanks on the time line. Two events are filled in for you.

Since the time the American Revolution began in 1776, the people of France and the United States have been friends. In 1865, A Frenchman suggested building a statue as a gift from the people of France to the people of the United States. The French people would pay for the statue. The people of the United States would pay for the base on which it would stand.

The enormous statue was made of copper in many sections to be reassembled in the United States. The statue was presented to the American Minister in Paris on July 4, 1884. It was then shipped in 214 crates to New York City in May 1885. By October 1886, it was assembled and dedicated as the Statue of Liberty by President Grover Cleveland.

Floodlights were added to the statue's base in 1916. The statue became a national monument eight years later. In 1956, the island on which the statue stands was renamed Liberty Island.

1. _____ American Revolution began.

2. _____ A Frenchman suggested building a statue.

3. _1884_ The statue was presented to American Minister in Paris.

4. _____ The statue was shipped to New York City.

5. _____ President Cleveland dedicated the Statue of Liberty.

6. _____ Floodlights were added to the base.

7. _____ The Statue of Liberty became a national monument.

8. _1956_ The island was renamed.

USING A TIME LINE TO FOLLOW SEQUENCE OF MAIN IDEAS

ELEPHANTS AT WORK

Keeping track of the dates in a selection will help you follow the main ideas. A time line is a good device for noting the order in which events happen.

> Read the selection. Then, on the time line, fill in the date that goes with each sentence. The first one is done for you.

Asian elephants are known for their superior brains and peaceful dispositions. They have been trained to help people since before the year 3,500 B.C. If treated properly, they serve their human friends well. Trained elephants have filled three important roles. They have been warriors, workers, and circus performers.

Written records show that the Egyptians were the first people to tame African elephants. The Egyptians tamed elephants in 300 B.C. The African general Hannibal used warrior elephants in his fight against the Roman Empire in 218 B.C. The elephants were brought from Africa to Europe by ship. The huge beasts managed to cross the snow-covered Alps carrying heavy loads. Then they were used in battle against the Romans.

Elephants were used in warfare as recently as 1862. At that time, the King of Siam (now Thailand) offered President Lincoln some of his best fighting elephants to use in the Civil War. Lincoln politely turned down the offer. Perhaps he realized the elephants would have been of little use against guns.

Even though elephants are no longer used in battles, people's interest in these animals is far from over. Elephants have often been captured and brought to zoos where thousands of people could see them.

One of the most famous elephants of all times, Jumbo, was brought to the London Zoo in 1865. He was the largest elephant ever captured. His name became a word in the English language, *jumbo,* meaning very large. Despite his size, he was as gentle as a pony. English children loved him because he gave them rides as they sat in a basket on his back. In 1882, Jumbo was sold to an American circus and sent to the United States. There, he became famous as the world's biggest elephant. At every circus performance, he attracted thousands of people who wanted to see him.

Three years after his arrival in the United States, Jumbo was in a terrible accident. As his keeper led him across a seldom-used railroad track, a speeding freight train struck him and killed him instantly.

Today, elephants are still used as workers to move logs and other heavy loads in the jungles of Asia. And, of course, what would the circus be without elephants?

1. **3,500 BC** Elephants were first trained in India.

2. **300 BC** African elephants were tamed.

3. **216 B** Elephants were used to fight the Romans.

4. **1862** President Lincoln was offered elephants for war.

5. **1865** Jumbo was brought to the London Zoo.

6. **1882** Jumbo was sold to an American circus.

7. **1885** Jumbo was killed in a railroad accident.

8. **Today** Elephants are used for moving logs and in circuses.

USING A TIME LINE TO FOLLOW SEQUENCE OF MAIN IDEAS

YELLOW HAIR

A time line lets you keep track of the order in which things happen.

> Read the selection. Look at the time line that follows. In this exercise, the dates are given, but not the events. Next to each date on the time line write a sentence that tells what happened for that date.

George Armstrong Custer was born in 1839 and died in 1876, but those thirty-seven years were packed with adventure. As a boy, George dreamed of becoming a soldier. That dream came true in 1861, the year he was graduated from the U.S. Military Academy at West Point at the age of twenty-one.

During the Civil War, Custer served as a cavalry officer and was involved in many battles. He was promoted to general in 1863, when he was only twenty-three years old.

USING A TIME LINE TO FIND MAIN IDEAS

After the war, Custer remained in the army and led troops against the Indians of the West. The Indians had their own name for Custer. They called him Yellow Hair because of his blond hair.

American settlers were pushing into the Sioux and Cheyenne hunting grounds. These tribes joined to fight to keep their land. Custer and his troops were part of a larger force that was supposed to attack the Indians.

On June 22, 1876, without waiting for the rest of the army to catch up to his troops, Custer led his men into Sioux territory. He planned to trap the Indians and defeat them with just the six hundred men he commanded. He did not realize that the Indians outnumbered his soldiers by at least five to one. Custer divided his men into three columns and led one column himself. On June 25, Custer crossed the Little Bighorn River and attacked the main Sioux camp.

Custer's scouts had warned him of the huge number of warriors he faced. The scouts had suggested that he wait until the rest of the army could catch up with him, but he did not listen.

The Sioux, led by Chief Crazy Horse, had set a trap. Their enemy, Yellow Hair, rode right into it. The battle ended on June 26. The only survivor from Custer's column was one cavalry horse.

In 1946, Congress made the Custer Battlefield at the Little Bighorn River a national monument.

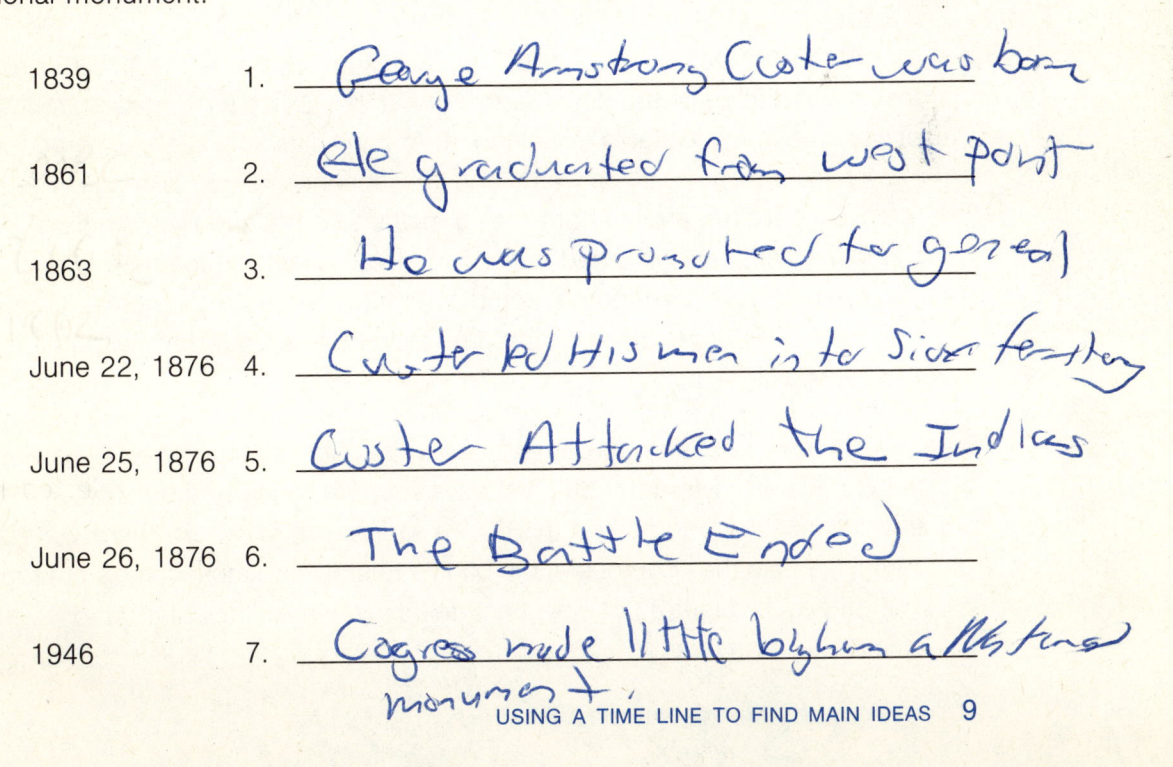

1839	1.	*George Armstrong Custer was born*
1861	2.	*He graduated from West Point*
1863	3.	*He was promoted to general*
June 22, 1876	4.	*Custer led his men into Sioux territory*
June 25, 1876	5.	*Custer attacked the Indians*
June 26, 1876	6.	*The battle ended*
1946	7.	*Congress made little bighorn a national monument*

USING A TIME LINE TO FIND MAIN IDEAS

THE CAMELS ARE COMING!

Writers use **time markers** to accomplish two goals. Time markers help the reader keep track of the order in which events in a story take place. They also call attention to the main ideas. Some time markers are listed below.

after	**finally**	**now**
at about the same time	**first**	**second**
at last	**formerly**	**simultaneously**
at the start	**in the beginning**	**soon**
before	**last**	**then**
began	**later**	**toward the end**
during	**meanwhile**	**while**
earlier	**next**	**while this was going on**

> Read the article. Circle each time marker you find. Then follow the directions on page 11.

A.   About ten years before the Civil War, the United States had to protect towns and settlers in the desert areas of the West. This territory included parts of what are now the states of California, Arizona, Nevada, Utah, Colorado, and New Mexico. The lack of water and the absence of roads made it almost impossible for the army's horses and mules to carry supplies. A young army officer had an idea. He urged the army to experiment with camels. Camels, he pointed out, were sure-footed, could carry heavier loads than horses or mules, and could also cover three hundred miles in three to four days without having food or water.

B.   There was not a single camel in the United States at the time. At the start of the experiment, two army officers were sent out to learn about camels. They traveled to the London Zoo in Britain, to Pisa, Italy, where there were 250 camels, and to the countries of the Middle East, where most camels are found. The officers brought 33 camels back to Texas, where they started to train the animals for army use.

C.   In the beginning, most people laughed at the strange-looking beasts. Soon, however, people changed their tune when the camels began to show what they could do. Camels carried 600 to 1200 pounds (272–544 kilograms) on their backs. They traveled 65 miles (105 kilometers) in eight hours. One camel went without water for ten days and then refused a drink of water. Finally, the experiment was declared a success. The army ordered a thousand camels. Meanwhile, the Civil War broke out, and the order was canceled.

D.   The original group of camels brought to the United States was sold off to circus and freight companies, and some were turned loose in the desert. Some of the children and grandchildren of these camels lived wild in the desert for almost a hundred years. The last wild camel was seen about fifty years ago.

> Read the sentences below. They are not in the same order as in the article. Place them in the order in which they happened by writing 1 next to the first event, 2 next the second, and so on. The first one is done for you.

a. _____ A young officer had the idea of using camels.

b. _____ The experiment was declared a success.

c. ___1___ The United States had to protect towns and settlers.

d. _____ Most people laughed when they saw the camels.

e. _____ The camels showed what they could do.

f. _____ Thirty-three camels were brought to Texas.

g. _____ The Civil War prevented the importing of camels.

h. _____ The camels were sold or turned loose.

USING TIME MARKERS TO FIND MAIN IDEAS

TIME CAPSULES

Add-ons are terms that let us know that other important facts are coming. Add-ons signal us to look for main ideas. Some add-ons are listed below.

also	in addition
and	(even) more important
another	moreover
besides	more than that
for example	then
for instance	too
further	similarly
furthermore	specifically

Read the article through once. Then go back and circle each add-on as you find it. Finally, use the add-ons to help you complete the sentences on page 13.

A.   In 1939, a group of people at the New York World's Fair built and buried something they called a time capsule. This ten-foot (3-meter) long copper tube that was lowered deep into the earth looked like a torpedo. It was not to be opened for five thousand years. It contained a strange assortment of objects. For example, it had a telephone, some coins, recordings, a Bible, a novel, baseball cards, and a toothbrush. Even more important, there was, on film, the story of our civilization and its achievements up to that time.

B.   To be sure that people living five thousand years from now will know where to find the capsule, *The Book of Record* was distributed around the world. This book was printed on special paper with ink that will never fade. The book describes the project and also tells how to decode the English language. Thousands of copies have been placed all over the world in the hope that people of the future will find it and recover the capsule.

C.   Although the World's Fair capsule is the most famous, it is by no means the first and, moreover, certainly will not be the last. For many years, people have been burying another kind of capsule. They have placed small safes in the cornerstones of buildings. These hollow stone blocks are placed in buildings that are under construction. Most of these cornerstone capsules contained a newspaper, photos, and stamps and coins. Besides these items, some have a letter addressed to the people who might dig up the box. In addition to the cornerstone capsules, there have been a few very strange messages to the future. One capsule holds a car with a full tank of gasoline. The capsule is to be opened in the year 2007. You may be the lucky one to find the car and drive it away.

D.   You may want to make your own time capsule. Items buried in a tightly sealed container would last a long time. For instance, you could put in coins, stamps, trading cards, and toys. More than that, you may want to put in some photos showing how either you or your school looks today.

1. The capsule buried at the New York World's Fair contained strange objects. For example, it had _____ _____.

2. Even more important, the capsule had on film _____ _____.

3. Another kind of capsule was _____ _____.

4. In addition to time capsules and cornerstones, one strange message to the future is _____.

5. In your own capsule you might, for instance, put in _____ _____.

USING ADD-ONS TO FIND MAIN IDEAS   13

KEYBOARD GENIUS

Summarizers and **concluders** are signal words and phrases that help us bring together thoughts that form main ideas. Some summarizers and concluders are listed below.

apparently	**in conclusion**	**so**	**we can see**
as a result	**in effect**	**therefore**	**we have demonstrated**
clearly	**in summary**	**thus**	**we have shown**
consequently	**obviously**		

> Read the selection. Circle the summarizers and concluders. Then use these to complete the sentences that follow the selection.

A. Tom Wiggins, who lived a hundred years ago, was a genius of the piano keyboard. Wiggins was the son of a slave. When he was born, Tom was totally blind. As Wiggins grew up, he developed an unusual gift. Although he could neither read Braille nor add numbers, he could play on the piano any music he heard. Even if Wiggins heard a piece of music only once, he was able to play it perfectly. It did not matter whether the music was a child's nursery tune or a symphony, Wiggins could play it without any mistakes. Apparently, Wiggins was so accurate that when somebody made a mistake in playing a piece, Wiggins would repeat the error when he played it back. Wiggins's genius was clearly demonstrated by the fact that he could play in the exact style of any great piano player he had ever heard.

B. Obviously, with the ability Wiggins had, it was not long before he went into show business and played in concert halls all over America and Europe. We can see that Wiggins was a genius, but the strange thing was that he had never seen a piano, had never been taught to play, nor had he received any training in music. Apparently, he was not even interested in music. In some strange way, Tom Wiggins's brain was able to record every note it heard. As a result, his fingers were directed to the correct piano keys. In effect, he was a true genius, but we do not understand how his gift worked.

1. Wiggins could play back any music he ever heard. Apparently, he was so accurate that when somebody made a playing error _____ _____.

2. Wiggins's talent led him to make his living by _____ _____.

3. We can see that the strange thing about Wiggins's genius was that he _____.

4. In effect, Wiggins was a true genius, but _____ _____.

A GIANT FAKE

A **both-sides signal** calls attention to the ideas that come before it and also to the ideas that come after it. The ideas that come after are restated with a different point of view. Some both-sides signals are listed below.

although	by contrast		
anyhow	despite	in fact	nevertheless
besides	even though	in particular	on the other hand
but	however	instead	yet

> Read the selection. Circle every both-sides signal that you find. Then follow the directions on page 17.

A. Two workers who were digging a well uncovered a fantastic discovery. Their digging revealed what they were sure was the body of a man turned to stone. The stone giant was over ten feet (3 meters) tall and weighed three thousand pounds (1,361 kilograms). The discovery took place in Cardiff, New York. The stone figure became known as the Cardiff Giant.

B. Experts who were called in to examine the Giant declared that it was truly a fossil man. Despite the experts' statements, some people did not believe that the Giant had ever lived. They claimed it was a figure that someone had carved out of stone. Nevertheless, people came from all over and paid to see the Giant. The famous circus showman, P. T. Barnum, wanted to rent the Giant to build a show around him. The farmer who owned the Giant refused Barnum's offer. Barnum, however, could not be stopped. Instead of the original Giant, Barnum had a sculptor make a copy for him. Even though people knew that Barnum's Giant was a copy, they were willing to pay their money to see it.

C. Newspaper reporters investigated the story of the original Giant. They found that the farmer's partner had bought a large block of stone in another state. He had hired a stonecutter to shape the stone and ship it to Cardiff. The partner finally admitted that, in fact, the Giant was a fake. The partner told how he aged the block of stone by using ink, sand, and acid. He had given the Giant's skin pores by hammering darning needles into it. Then, although the Giant looked real, they buried it anyhow for a year before arranging for it to be "accidentally" discovered.

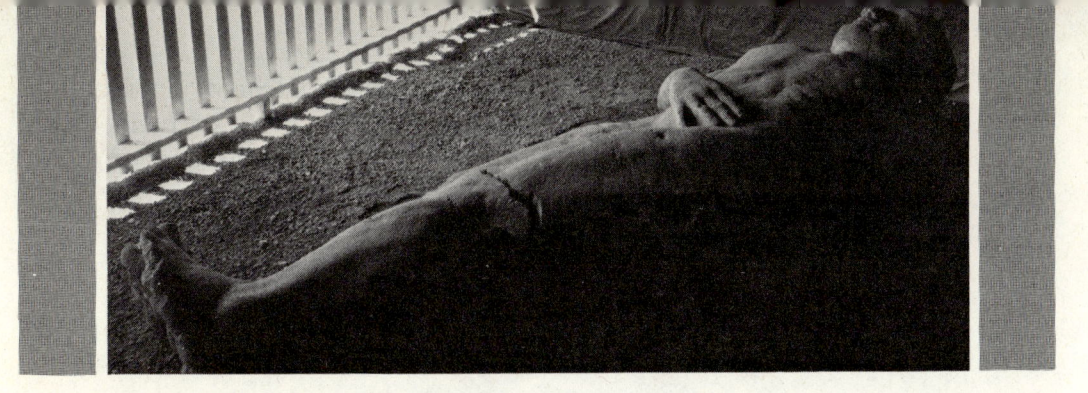

The Giant was a fake, but, on the other hand, it fooled many of the experts. Barnum was right when he said, "There's a sucker born every minute."

> In each sentence below, circle the both-sides signal that fits best.

    Despite
1. However   the experts, some people did not believe the Giant had lived.
    Moreover

    In particular
2. Instead   people came from all over and paid to see the Giant.
    Nevertheless

           besides,
3. Barnum, instead, could not be stopped.
           however,

    Even though
4. In particular people knew Barnum's was a copy, they paid to see it.
    On the other hand

                    although,
5. The partner finally admitted that, in fact, the Giant was a fake.
                    despite,

    Nevertheless
6. Moreover   the Giant looked real, they still buried it for a year.
    Although

USING BOTH-SIDES SIGNALS TO FIND MAIN IDEAS

YANKEE DOODLE

Pointers are signal words or phrases that indicate important points or main ideas. Some pointer words are listed below.

chief	**mainly**	**primarily**
chiefly	**most**	**principal**
especially	**most important**	**principally**

Read the selection. Circle the pointers as you find them. Then follow the directions on page 19.

        Yankee Doodle went to town,
           A-riding on a pony,
        Stuck a feather in his hat
          And called it macaroni.

        Yankee Doodle keep it up.
        Yankee Doodle dandy.
        Mind the music and the step,
        And with the girls be handy.

A.   Have you ever whistled or sung the song "Yankee Doodle"? This great American song was written as an English tune primarily to make fun of Americans. The original words of the song were written by a British Army doctor in the years before the Revolutionary War. In the days when American colonials marched beside British soldiers to fight the French and Indians, the colonials made a poor showing. The Americans, with their fur hats and leather shirts and pants, wore an odd combination of uniforms compared to the British in their beautiful red coats and white belts. The colonials were especially angry at the song because they thought that they were better soldiers than the British.

B.   As the years went by, the Americans adopted the song and made it their own. By the time the Revolutionary War began, "Yankee Doodle" was the American Army's principal tune. The Americans delighted in playing the song at the British defeats at Concord, Bunker Hill, and the Battle of Saratoga. It was played as a victory song when the British Army surrendered at Yorktown to end the war.

USING POINTERS TO FIND MAIN IDEAS

C.   "Yankee Doodle" became the most important national song to come out of the Revolutionary War period.

> Complete the sentences below. Use the pointers in the selection to help you find the important ideas they indicate.

1. "Yankee Doodle" was written primarily _____
   _____.

2. The colonials were especially angry because _____
   _____.

3. The principal tune of the American Army _____.

4. "Yankee Doodle" became the most important _____
   _____.

USING POINTERS TO FIND MAIN IDEAS   19

A THREE-HUNDRED-YEAR-OLD SECRET

This selection uses many different kinds of signal words and phrases. Some of the signal words that you know belong to the following groups.

- time markers
- add-ons
- summarizers and concluders
- both-sides signals
- pointers

> Read the story. Then use your knowledge of signal words to choose the correct term from each group of three. Circle the correct term.

A.   Today every serious violinist would like to own a Stradivarius violin. Why? The violins that were made by Antonio Stradivari three hundred years ago are the world's most wonderful instruments because of their glorious tones and because they are *nevertheless / also / however* the most beautiful violins ever made.

B.   *Now / Since / After* working as an apprentice violin-maker for many years, Stradivari opened his own shop when he was thirty-six years old.

His *principal / further / earlier* goal was to make his violins sing like a human voice.

In the beginning / Toward the end / On the other hand Stradivari built violins with many different shapes until he found the shape that had the best tone. Within four years, he was a well-known and wealthy man. *Anyhow, / In fact, / However,* he never told anyone the

20   USING SIGNAL WORDS TO FIND MAIN IDEAS

secret of his success.

C.   Besides
We have seen Stradivari's two sons worked in his shop,
Even though
he never told them his secret. Many other violin-makers
moreover
copied the shape, but   they could never get the tone of a Stradivarius.
thus
Some people believed that the tone resulted from the wood Stradivari used. Others thought the sound came from the special sap of trees he
Previously
used in assembling his instruments. Meanwhile modern chemists
After
analyzed the varnish coating of the violins, most experts concluded
In fact,
that it was the varnish that made the chief difference. By contrast,
We can see,
Stradivari's great-grandson said that he discovered his grandfather's secret formula for varnish in an old family Bible. Even though he was
In conclusion
poor, the great-grandson refused to part with the secret. In effect
As a result
of the chemists' discovery, some violin-makers have been able to improve the tone of their violins by copying the varnish.

D.   Clearly
Despite   this improvement, the copiers are still a long way
Likewise
from capturing the sound of a genuine Stradivarius. The secret of Antonio Stradivari's violins remains almost as much a mystery today as it was three hundred years ago.

DISCOVERERS OF THE NORTH POLE

Discovering which words belong in the blank spaces will help you find the main ideas.

> Choose the word from each group that makes the most sense. Write it in the blank. Then circle the letter of the statement that best expresses the main idea of each paragraph.

Robert Peary lived for many years with one ambition—to be the first person to discover the North Pole. He spent twenty years preparing for the great trip. He studied the Eskimos' ways of _____ , and he explored the Arctic region. He thought that if he discovered the North Pole, he would be as famous as Christopher Columbus.

1. writing
   traveling
   cooking

A. a. Robert Peary enjoyed Eskimo living.
   b. Robert Peary was a great admirer of Christopher Columbus.
   c. Robert Peary spent twenty years preparing for his trip.

Peary had made several attempts to reach the North Pole, but _____ weather stopped him each time. Finally, in 1909, he made his successful journey to the Pole. The final expedition included six Americans, seventeen Eskimos, and nineteen sleds pulled by 133 sled dogs. As supplies were used up, sled after sled dropped out to _____ to the base. After traveling 300 miles (483 kilometers), just a handful of men remained to attempt the final 100-mile (161-kilometer) trip. They were Peary, Mathew Henson, his friend of many years, and four Eskimos.

2. bad
   good
   cold

3. circle
   return
   continue

B. a. Peary needed many dogs for the trip.
   b. Peary was about to realize his goal.
   c. As supplies were used up, the sleds returned.

USING CLOZE TO FIND MAIN IDEAS IN PARAGRAPHS

Admiral Peary, center; Matthew Henson, left and right

At last, Peary and his team reached the North Pole. Even though the men were exhausted, Peary and Henson were overjoyed. Peary wrote in his diary, "The Pole at last! My dream and _____4_____ of twenty years. Mine at last!" They planted the American flag and buried a bottle with a message claiming the North Pole for the United States. After spending a night at the Pole, they returned to the base camp.

Although others claimed to have reached the North Pole before Peary and Henson, the United States Congress recognized them as having reached the Pole _____5_____. Peary's book, *The North Pole*, is a convincing record that he was really the first to reach the North Pole.

4. goal
   nightmare
   fear

5. last
   soon
   first

C. a. Everyone believed that Peary discovered the North Pole.
   b. Peary wrote a convincing book.
   c. Congress recognized Peary's claim.

USING CLOZE TO FIND MAIN IDEAS IN PARAGRAPHS

WHEN BIGGER IS BETTER

Deciding which word fits the blank space will help you find the main idea of an article.

> Choose the word from each group that makes the most sense. Write it in the blank. Then follow the directions on page 25.

A.   R. Buckminster Fuller is an unusual name, and the buildings he designs are also unusual. Some people think that Fuller's _____1_____ may be the most important new idea in construction in the last hundred years. Interestingly enough, the shape of Fuller's buildings is copied from nature. The shape is like a half bubble sitting on a table top, with a round top and a flat bottom. The buildings are called geodesic (jee-uh-DESS-ik) domes.

1. name
   buildings
   life

B.   Because of the way the _____2_____ are built, they are stronger when they are bigger. The bigger the dome, the stronger the building. This means that huge domes could be built. In fact, there is no limit to the size a dome can be. Some people can imagine the day when a whole city could be covered by a single dome. The weather inside the dome could be _____3_____. If we had the time and money, we could even cover a whole desert area like the Sahara. Or, the frozen Arctic could be _____4_____ over and warmed up. Then, people could grow food and live there. Thousands of geodesic domes have already been built all over the world. The sizes of the buildings range from ten feet (3 meters) across to almost a half mile (804 meters) across.

2. domes
   bubbles
   tops

3. unpleasant
   unknown
   controlled

4. covered
   cooled
   passed

USING CLOZE TO FIND THE MAIN IDEA

C.   Someday, perhaps domes will make it possible

for people to _____ on the moon.   5. land
                      5   live
There is no air on the moon. A moon city built   travel
under a dome, however, could make its own air, and
the bubble top would keep it in. It is possible that you
or your children may live in a dome-shaped house that
is part of a dome-shaped city on the moon.

> Circle the letter of the sentence that best tells the main idea of each paragraph. Finally, circle the letter of the best title for the article.

A. a. The dome may be the most important idea in construction in the last one hundred years.
    b. R. Buckminster Fuller is an unusual name.
    c. The dome looks like a bubble.

B. a. Time and money determine the size of a building.
    b. Deserts and frozen lands have been covered with domes.
    c. There is no limit to the size of a dome that can be built.

C. a. There are bubble tops on the moon.
    b. The moon is dome shaped.
    c. Someday people may live under domes on the moon.

D. The best title for the article is:
    a. "Copying from Nature"
    b. "A New Kind of Building"
    c. "An Unusual Man with an Unusual Name"

PIGEON POWER

If you can learn to find the missing words, you will become better at finding main ideas.

> Choose the word from each group that makes the most sense. Write it in the blank. Then circle the letter of the sentence that best tells the main idea of each paragraph. Finally, pick the best title for the article.

A. Some of the greatest heroes of World War I were carrier pigeons. These birds were trained to carry _____ in a tiny capsule
₁
attached to one of their legs. During the war, a group of American soldiers fighting in France were completely surrounded by the _____.
₂
The soldiers were far away from the rest of the American Army and unable to get help. They had no radio, telegraph, or telephone. Several brave soldiers tried unsuccessfully to get through the enemy lines. The remaining soldiers were out of food and ammunition. Only one hope remained. They had brought four carrier pigeons with them. The soldiers sent out three _____ with
₃
messages asking for help. When no help came, the soldiers knew that the birds had not gotten through. There was only one pigeon left to go for help. Its name was Cher Ami, which means "dear friend" in French.

1. troops
   messages
   pigeons

2. enemy
   pigeons
   French

3. letters
   telegrams
   pigeons

B. When they tossed Cher Ami into the air, the bird flew high and straight for the _____
₄
camp. The message it carried saved the endangered

4. French
   American
   enemy

26   USING CLOZE TO FIND THE MAIN IDEA

soldiers. For this deed, Cher Ami was awarded a medal for heroism.

C.   With today's marvelous communications, you might think that carrier pigeons would no longer be useful as message carriers. However, one of the largest missile and aircraft manufacturing companies in the United States uses a pigeon system to fly plans from one factory to another. At one factory, the plans are reduced and _____ 5 onto a tiny piece of film. The film is tucked into a _____ 6 just like the one used by Cher Ami. When the pigeons reach the second factory, the film is enlarged to its original size. Since the factories are separated by fifty miles (80 kilometers) of mountainous roads, the pigeons save the company considerable time and money. Carrier pigeons continue to show how valuable they can be, even in the modern world.

5. photographed
   drawn
   painted

6. camera
   factory
   capsule

A. a. During World War I, American soldiers fought in France.
    b. Pigeons were important for carrying messages.
    c. The American soldiers were without radios, telegraphs, or telephones.

B. a. Cher Ami saved the soldiers.
    b. Cher Ami flew high and straight.
    c. Cher Ami was awarded a medal.

C. a. Today's pigeons use capsules like those used by Cher Ami.
    b. Today, plans can be reduced to a tiny piece of film.
    c. Carrier pigeons are still useful today.

D. The best title for the story is:
    a. "A Battle of World War I"
    b. "How To Fly Plans over Mountains"
    c. "A Helpful Bird"

USING CLOZE TO FIND THE MAIN IDEA

THE HIGHWAYMAN WAS A WOMAN

Writers use patterns to organize their thoughts. The more you know about patterns, the better you will be able to follow a writer's ideas.

One kind of writing pattern is called the **problem-solution pattern.** It has four steps.

1. The problem is recognized and stated.
2. A solution is suggested.
3. The steps in solving the problem are given.
4. There is proof that the solution is a good one.

> Read the selection. Use the statements at the end of the article to complete the outline of the problem-solution pattern.

In the early sixteenth century, English kings ruled Scotland. Many Scots were opposed to the rule of English kings. To try to put down the opposition, the kings often arrested people who they thought were against them. Sometimes the people who were arrested were put to death. Often, the mere suspicion of disloyalty to the king was enough to have people imprisoned or put to death.

Sir John was one such prisoner of the king. He was under sentence of death because the king thought that Sir John had been disloyal. When Sir John's wife and daughter visited him in prison, they learned that the sentence would probably be carried out very soon. The prison warden explained that when the order with the king's signature arrived, the prison authorities would carry out the sentence. The warden expected the messenger to arrive with the order the next morning.

Gizelle, Sir John's daughter, believed that the king could be convinced that her father should be freed. Her problem was how to get to the king before the death sentence could be carried out. If only the messenger delivering the order could be stopped!

In those days, there were masked riders called highwaymen who robbed people on the roads at night. That evening, a highwayman held up the messenger carrying Sir John's death sentence and stole all the official papers. Without the order, the sentence could not be carried out. A search was made, but the highwayman was never found.

The delay succeeded. Sir John's family was able to convince the king to free the brave Scot. Little did anyone ever suspect or know that the highwayman was really a girl—Sir John's daughter, Gizelle.

A. Problem: _____
_____
_____

B. Solution: _____
_____
_____

C. Steps that led to the solution:

1. _____
_____

2. _____
_____

3. _____
_____

D. Proof that the solution worked:
_____
_____

- The messenger could not deliver the order for Sir John's death.

- Time was needed to reach the king before the sentence could be carried out.

- Gizelle disguised herself as a masked highwayman.

- Gizelle stole the papers with the death sentence.

- Sir John's life was saved.

- Gizelle held up the messenger.

USING THE PROBLEM-SOLUTION PATTERN TO FIND MAIN IDEAS

LIFE FROM LIFE

Knowing the problem-solution pattern will help you follow a writer's ideas. Remember the four steps in the pattern.

1. statement of the problem
2. statement of the solution
3. steps in the solution
4. proof that the solution works

Read the selection. Then fill in the blanks in your own words. Use ideas from the story.

Years ago, most people believed in the spontaneous generation of life. "Spontaneous" means happening all by itself. "Generation" refers to the start of new life. People who believed in spontaneous generation thought that nonliving things could come to life all by themselves. These people believed that worms could come to life by themselves from horsehairs placed in water. They also thought that frogs could come from mud and that rotting meat turned into flies.

"Nonsense!" said Lazzaro Spallanzani (spah-lahn-ZAH-nee), an Italian who lived at the time of George Washington. "Worms do not come from horsehairs. Worms come from other worms who are their parents. Frogs come from other frogs, and flies come from other flies. Living things come only from living things."

"You'll have to prove that!" people said. Spallanzani did just that.

Spallanzani placed pieces of clean meat in three different glass jars. The first jar was open at the top. Air could get at the meat, and so could flies. The second jar had a tightly covered lid. No air or flies could get at the meat inside the jar. The third jar was covered with a piece of screening which allowed air but no flies to get at the meat.

"So what?" said the people who believed that flies came by spontaneous generation from nonliving things. "What are you trying to prove? There are no flies on any of the pieces of meat."

"Just wait," said Spallanzani.

In a little while, there was something to see. The meat in the jar that was open at the top was crawling with maggots—the wormlike forms of baby flies.

"See!" said the people who believed in spontaneous generation. "Flies do come from rotting meat."

"But look at the covered jar," said Spallanzani. "The meat is rotten, but there are no flies on it. And look at the jar with the screening. There are flies' eggs on the top of the screening, but there are no maggots in the meat. See? Flies come from other flies, not from rotten meat. The flies that could get at the meat laid eggs on the meat, and the eggs developed into maggots. On the jars where no flies could get at the meat, there are no maggots. On the jar with the screening, flies tried to lay eggs on the meat. But there are no maggots on that meat because the flies could not get to the meat."

"We guess you are right," agreed many people. "Living things come only from living things."

Problem: Spallanzani wanted to show that _____

_____

Solution: Spallanzani showed people that flies _____

_____

Steps in the Solution: Spallanzani set out three jars of meat. One was

_____1_____. Another was _____2_____.

The third was _____3_____.

Proof: The only meat that had maggots on it was from the jar that _____4_____

_____

USING THE PROBLEM-SOLUTION PATTERN TO FIND MAIN IDEAS 31

A PROBLEM WITH ICE

The problem-solution pattern helps you follow a writer's organization. This selection follows a slightly different form of the pattern. Sometimes the writer may describe some solutions that did not work. Then the pattern looks like this.

1. The problem is stated.
2. Possible solutions (that did not work) are given.
3. The solution that did work is stated.
4. There is proof that the solution is a good one.

Read the selection. Then fill in the blanks with your own words. Use the ideas you read about in the story.

In the early days of aviation, icing—the build-up of ice on an airplane's wings—was no problem. Back then, airplanes flew low, and they flew only when the weather was good. Then, in the days following World War I, some airplanes began to carry passengers and mail. These airplanes had to fly on a strict schedule. That meant sometimes they would have to fly in freezing temperatures. The mail had to go through, even if there was ice at high altitudes. The mail planes had to fly at high altitudes because in crossing the United States between New York and California, they had to fly over the Rocky Mountains. Often, the aircraft wings would develop thick layers of ice.

Icing on the wings creates two dangerous conditions. First, because ice is very heavy, it can weigh the plane down and cause it to crash. Second, the ice that forms on the wings freezes in a layer that covers the outside controls. That makes it impossible for the airplane to turn or to climb. In the old days, about the only thing a pilot could do if his plane started to ice up was to change altitude. If the pilot flew lower, the plane might strike warmer air that would melt the ice. The trouble with flying lower was that the plane might hit a mountain.

Different ideas were tried for melting the ice. Hot exhaust gasses from the engine were directed toward the wings. The hot gasses helped, but they did not prevent the icing. Placing electric heating wires on the wings did not help much either.

Then a very simple scheme was developed. A de-icer, a flat rubber tube, was placed along the front edge of the wing. When there was no ice, it remained flat on the wing and out of the way. When ice began to form, the pilot would start a small pump. The pump inflated the de-icer and then let the air out so that the de-icer deflated. Each time the de-icer inflated, it broke up the ice on the front edges of the wing. The onrushing air then would get under the ice and blow it away.

Every airplane manufactured today has a de-icer. Even the biggest jumbo jets depend on the little rubber tubes to keep the planes flying when there is icy weather.

Problem: When planes flew in freezing weather, _____
_____.

Possible solutions that did not work: Before there were good de-icers,

the only thing a pilot could do was to _____1_____.

Hot engine exhaust gasses _____2_____,

but they did not work very well. _____3_____ placed on the wings did

not help much either.

Solution that worked: The ice on the front edge of the wing is broken up by
_____.

Proof that it worked: _____.

USING THE PROBLEM-SOLUTION PATTERN TO FIND MAIN IDEAS 33

AN AMERICAN SUCCESS STORY

An **outline** is the basic plan of an article or story. Outlining shows how main ideas and supporting details fit together. Outlining helps you organize your thoughts.

> Read the selection. Then complete the outline by filling in the blanks. Choose your answers from the list of main ideas and details at the end of the selection.

Romana Acosta Bañuelos was born in Arizona in 1925, but she grew up in Mexico. When Mrs. Bañuelos was twenty-four years old, she bought a tortilla stand in Los Angeles. She paid $400 for the stand. The tiny tortilla stand grew into a large company. So many of her customers called her Ramona instead of Romana that she called her company by the name most of her customers were using. She called it Ramona's Mexican Food Products, Inc.

By 1970, Ramona's Mexican Food Products was selling Mexican food all over southern California and in other states as well. She employed more than one hundred fifty workers, most of them Mexican-Americans. In just nine short years, the company that had started as a little tortilla stand had more than four hundred employees. Both of Mrs. Bañuelos's sons were vice presidents of the company.

While Romana Bañuelos was building a successful company, she also helped other Mexican-Americans succeed. She organized a bank in East Los Angeles. At the time, the bank was the only one in the United States completely owned and operated by Mexican-Americans. She started a scholarship program that made it possible for many Mexican-American students to go to college.

A high point in Romana Bañuelos's life was her appointment as Treasurer of the United States from 1971 to 1974. She was the first Mexican-American woman appointed to such an important position. As Treasurer, she signed checks for all money spent by the United States government and she supervised the destruction of worn-out money. Her signature appeared on all the paper money printed while she was Treasurer.

Romana Acosta Bañuelos succeeded in many areas of American life.

Main Ideas and Details

The tortilla stand grew into a large company.

Romana Bañuelos helped other Mexican Americans.

Romana Bañuelos became a successful businesswoman.

Her signature appeared on U.S. paper money.

She started a tortilla stand.

She started a college scholarship program.

She signed all United States government checks.

She supervised the destruction of worn-out money.

She was the first Mexican-American Treasurer of the United States.

I. _____
   (main idea)

  A. _____
     (detail)

  B. _____
     (detail)

    1. The business sold Mexican food all over southern California.
    2. The business employed 150 workers.
    3. The business grew to have 400 employees.

II. _____
   (main idea)

  A. She organized a bank.

  B. _____
     (detail)

III. Romana Acosta Bañuelos was appointed Treasurer of the United States.

  A. _____
     (detail)

  B. _____
     (detail)

  C. _____
     (detail)

  D. _____
     (detail)

USING AN OUTLINE TO FIND MAIN IDEAS

WHY SAVE THE WHALES?

Outlining will help you see how the main ideas of an article are organized. It will also show you how details support main ideas.

Read the selection. Complete the outline. Choose your answers from the list of main ideas and from the list of supporting details.

It is important that we maintain the balance of the entire food chain of the ocean. We do not know how the loss of one kind of animal or plant will affect the other living things in the ocean. It is especially important to save the whales because whales are in danger. Some kinds of whales are in danger of becoming extinct. The blue whale, the humpback, the right whale, and the sperm whale have been hunted until their numbers today are very small. Since we do not truly understand what effect our interference may have, it is only sensible to leave these great mammals alone. The actions we take today may disturb a natural balance about which we know very little. The things we do in ignorance may create problems for our children and their children. Something we destroy today will be gone forever.

There are even more selfish reasons for saving the whales. Human beings need protein in their diet. Whale meat is an important source of protein. Although today we get much of our protein from the meat of land animals and fish, the day may come when there are not enough land animals and fish. Then, if there are enough whales in the oceans of the world, we could turn to them for proteins. The whales would be there, and their meat would help the human race survive. They would survive only if we save them now.

There are also moral reasons for not killing off these great beasts. Whales are gentle creatures. They travel in family groups and they take good care of their young. Whales are very intelligent mammals. They make up songs and can communicate across great distances through their songs. Captive whales have learned to perform complex tricks. Many scientists believe that whales are only slightly less intelligent than humans.

Main Ideas

It is important to maintain the balance of the food chain.
There are selfish reasons for saving the whales.
There are moral reasons for not killing whales.

Supporting Details

We do not know what effect our interference will have on future life.
Some kinds of whales are in danger of becoming extinct.
Whales sing songs and communicate with each other.
Whales can perform complex tricks.
We may run short of protein from land animals and fish.
Whales care for their young.
Whales may be an important source of protein.
Whales travel in families.

I. _____
   (main idea)

  A. _____
     (detail)

  B. Blue, humpback, right, and sperm whales exist in very small numbers.

  C. _____
     (detail)

II. _____
   (main idea)

  A. People need protein.

  B. _____
     (detail)

  C. _____
     (detail)

III. _____
   (main idea)

  A. Whales are gentle animals.

    1. _____
       (detail)

    2. _____
       (detail)

  B. Whales are intelligent animals.

    1. _____
       (detail)

    2. _____
       (detail)

USING AN OUTLINE TO FIND MAIN IDEAS

FIRST LADY OF THE SKY

A **summary** is a short way of telling about something you have read. If you can write a summary, you know that you have understood the main idea.

> Read the selection. Put a check next to the phrase that best completes each sentence. Then, by using those phrases that give the main idea of each paragraph, complete the summary.

A. She had been a nurse's aide, a truck driver, a telephone operator, and a writer and editor. But Amelia Earhart loved flying best of all. During World War I, she worked in a military hospital caring for wounded pilots. They told her of their experiences in the air. She listened and decided to become a pilot. She was nineteen years old, and she lived during the time when there were almost no women pilots. Amelia Earhart learned to fly when she was twenty-one years old. By the age of twenty-four, she had saved enough money to buy her own airplane. In this plane she set a world altitude record by flying higher than any woman had ever flown before. She flew across the Atlantic Ocean with two men in 1928. In 1932, she became the first woman to fly across the Atlantic Ocean alone. She broke record after record as she flew higher, further, and faster than anyone else at that time.

B. For years, Amelia Earhart had one goal. She wanted to pilot a plane around the world. When asked why she wanted to break records, she said, "I want to do it because I must do it. Women must try to do things as men have tried."

C. Amelia Earhart started her 27,000-mile (43,443-kilometer) trip around the world with a navigator. They flew in a twin-engine airplane that could travel 4,000 miles (6,436 kilometers) before refueling. They started from Oakland, California, and flew on to Florida, Puerto Rico, Brazil, Africa, Pakistan, Burma, Singapore, Australia, and New Zealand. Then, misfortune struck. Partway between New Guinea and Howland Island in the Pacific, her plane began to run out of fuel.

D. She radioed the United States Coast Guard to give her probable location, but they could not hear her clearly. She sent one last message stating where she thought she was, and then her radio went dead. The navy searched for three weeks, but never found a trace of her or her navigator. That was the last anyone ever heard from Amelia Earhart, the first lady of the sky.

SUMMARIZING MAIN IDEAS

A. Amelia Earhart, an early woman pilot,
    ___ a. was a writer and editor.
    ___ b. set many records.
    ___ c. flew high, fast, and far.

B. Amelia Earhart's goal was to
    ___ a. break records.
    ___ b. do different things than men did.
    ___ c. pilot a plane around the world.

C. Even though her airplane could fly 4,000 miles (6,436 kilometers) without refueling, it
    ___ a. carried a navigator.
    ___ b. began to run out of fuel.
    ___ c. had two engines.

D. As her plane was going down, Amelia Earhart
    ___ a. radioed her probable position.
    ___ b. said goodbye to the Coast Guard radio operator.
    ___ c. requested that the navy search for her.

Amelia Earhart, an early woman pilot, _____1_____. Her goal was to _____2_____. Even though her plane could fly 4,000 miles (6,436 kilometers) without refueling, it _____3_____. As the plane was going down, Amelia Earhart _____4_____.

SUMMARIZING MAIN IDEAS   39

A STRANGE ZOO

If you understand the main ideas, you should be able to write a summary.

> Read each paragraph. Complete the summary with facts from the paragraph.

People of ancient times believed in a strange group of beasts that do not exist today and never existed then. Or did they?

At the top of the list of creatures that never really lived is the phoenix (FEE-nix). The ancient Egyptians described the phoenix as a red and gold bird the size of an eagle. It was said to fly into Egypt every five hundred years. The phoenix, according to legend, built a nest of sweet-smelling twigs, stepped into it, folded its wings, and burned itself up. From the ashes there would arise a new phoenix ready to repeat the whole process five hundred years later. The Romans heard about the phoenix. This story was so popular that the Romans adopted the phoenix and its flaming nest as the symbol for the royal family.

1. The phoenix renewed itself every five hundred years by building a nest

   and _____.

Another cage in this strange zoo of legendary creatures could be occupied by the unicorn. The unicorn looked like a white horse with a long, straight horn in the middle of its head. The unicorn was supposed to be powerful but gentle. Some people thought that its horn was magic. They believed that a cup made from the unicorn's horn could clean dirty water and make poisonous drinks harmless. The idea of the unicorn may have come from a small whale, the narwhal. The narwhal has a long, pointed ivory tusk growing out of its head. Many a narwhal has been killed for its horn, which was passed off as having come from a unicorn. Despite all the pictures of unicorns that have come down to us from ancient times, no such animal ever existed.

2. People believed that the unicorn's horn was valuable because it could

_____.

The griffin had the head and wings of an eagle joined to the body of a lion. It was sometimes called the flying lion. The griffin was thought to look like a real bird, the bearded vulture. It had a ten-foot (3-meter) wingspread and a four-foot (1.2-meter) body. To a person on the ground who saw a bearded vulture in the sky, it might indeed have looked like a flying lion. The real bearded vulture was found in Central Asia, North Africa, and Southern Europe. It is the people from these countries who believed in the imaginary creature called the griffin.

3. The griffin was called the flying lion because _____

_____.

SUMMARIZING MAIN IDEAS

UNFINISHED STORIES

Sometimes the main idea may not be stated in the materials you read. Often, the author gives you enough clues so that you can figure out the main idea for yourself. When you are able to find main ideas not directly stated, it will show that you are really a good reader.

> Read the selection. Put a check next to the unstated main idea. Then write three details from the story that support your choice of main ideas.

A. Captain Hawkins slid down the ladder. Sea water poured onto the metal deck beneath his feet.

"Take her down, emergency!" he ordered. A horn sounded.

"Dive! Dive!"

The crew scrambled to their diving stations.

Hawkins turned to his second-in-command, "There's an enemy ship coming straight at us. We've got to get down below five hundred feet where they can't pick us up with their sounding equipment."

Main Idea:

This story takes place on a

___ a. tanker.

___ b. submarine.

___ c. battleship.

Supporting Details:

1. _____.
2. _____.
3. _____.

42 INFERRING MAIN IDEAS AND LISTING SUPPORTING DETAILS

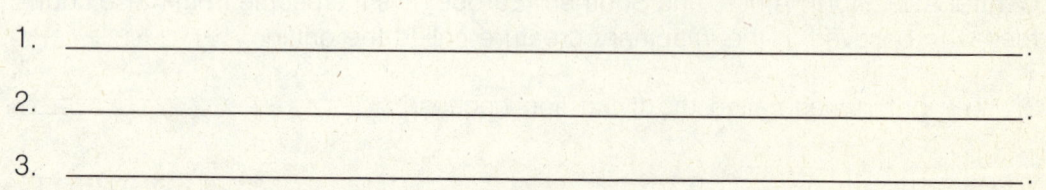

B.   "It must be 100° F. in the shade, and there's no shade within a hundred miles," said Ellen.

"I can't walk another step," said Steve. "We should have filled our gas tank and our canteens before we started. How far do you think we've come since we left the car?"

"I'm not sure," said Ellen. "But we've got to keep going. We must find help soon. Try to walk as far as you can, and then I'll carry you if I have to."

"Do you think anyone will find us?" Steve asked through cracked lips.

"Well, I wrote a note on my driver's license and put it on the front seat of the car. I told them which way we were heading. If someone finds the car, they may come after us or send help."

Main Idea:

Ellen and Steve

____ a. left their car to take a walk.

____ b. are on a hike and got lost.

____ c. are searching for help.

Supporting Details:

1. _____.

2. _____.

3. _____.

INFERRING MAIN IDEAS AND LISTING SUPPORTING DETAILS   43

YOU WRITE THE ENDING

Here is a story with enough clues for you to be able to figure out the ending.

> Read the selection. Put a check next to the ending that makes the most sense. Base your choice of the ending on details in the story. Then list four details that support your choice.

The castle had been under attack for weeks. It was completely surrounded and cut off from nearby friends. The enemy's war machines were now throwing large rocks. Cracks were beginning to appear in the castle walls. A battering ram was pounding at the main gate to the castle. A flaming arrow had started a fire that burned the last of the grain in the storehouse. Most of the water had been used to keep the flames from spreading. Now the brave defenders of the castle had only the few loaves of bread and the kettles of soup that had been in the kitchen. The soldiers on the walls were waiting for Little Margaret, the cook's helper, to bring them whatever food was left. They had learned to depend on her. This time, however, Margaret did not appear.

Soon the men began to call, "Margaret, Margaret." But their calls went unanswered.

44 PREDICTING THE MAIN IDEA AND FINDING SUPPORTING DETAILS

You don't think she ate the bread and is hiding, do you?" one soldier asked a knight.

"Margaret? Never!" answered the knight. "I've seen her share her own food with hungry men. Many times she gave her share of the water to the wounded. You stay here. I'll look for Margaret."

When the knight reached the kitchen, he found the bread and the soup waiting to be served. There was, however, no Margaret. Then, he noticed a hole in the kitchen wall. One of the huge rocks thrown by the enemy's war machines had caused a small crack in the wall. The opening was just wide enough for a small girl to slip through.

The knight returned to the soldier on the wall. "I think I know where Margaret has gone," he said.

Main idea:

Margaret has

_____ a. escaped to save herself.

_____ b. gone over to the enemy because she was hungry.

_____ c. gone through the crack in the wall to bring help.

Supporting Details:

1. _____

_____

2. _____

_____

3. _____

_____

4. _____

_____

PREDICTING THE MAIN IDEA AND FINDING SUPPORTING DETAILS

WHAT SHOULD BE DONE?

When a main idea is not directly stated, you should use the writer's clues to figure it out for yourself. Good readers can do this.

Read the selection. Then put a check next to the main idea. Write two details that support your choice.

The water-safety instructor began the course with the rules for helping a drowning person. She explained, "Here are the three basic procedures to keep in mind when a person is in danger of drowning: Throw, Row, Go Tow. First, when there is a long enough rope with a life preserver attached, throw it to the person. If you can't find a rope and life preserver or if you can't use it, look for a rowboat. Try to row out to the victim as quickly as possible. If neither a rope nor a boat is available, then you will have to swim out and tow in the person."

At the end of the summer, Suzanne visited her friend's home at Green Lake. Suddenly, she heard a cry, "Help! Help!" Far out in the middle of the big lake, someone was drowning. Suzanne looked around. There was nobody else in sight. She looked up and down the shore. There was a life preserver with a short rope attached to it. There was also a rowboat without any oars. Suzanne thought of what her water safety instructor had said. "I guess," thought Suzanne, "the best thing to do is . . ."

Main Idea:

The best thing that Suzanne can do is to

_____ a. throw.

_____ b. row.

_____ c. go tow.

Supporting Details:

1. _____

2. _____

46   INFERRING MAIN IDEAS AND LISTING SUPPORTING DETAILS

ANSWER KEY

Page 5
1. 1776
2. 1865
3. 1884
4. 1885
5. 1886
6. 1916
7. 1924
8. 1956

Pages 6 and 7
1. 3,500 B.C.
2. 300 B.C.
3. 218 B.C.
4. 1862
5. 1865
6. 1882
7. 1885
8. today

Pages 8 and 9
(Wording of answers may vary.)
1. Custer was born.
2. Custer was graduated from West Point.
3. Custer was promoted to general.
4. Custer led his men into Sioux territory.
5. Custer crossed the Little Bighorn River and attacked.
6. Custer and all his men died in the battle against the Sioux.
7. The Custer Battlefield was made a national monument.

Pages 10 and 11
A. About ten years before, now
B. at the time, At the start
C. In the beginning, Soon, in eight hours, for ten days, then, Finally, Meanwhile,
D. almost a hundred years, about fifty years ago

a. 2   e. 5
b. 6   f. 3
c. 1   g. 7
d. 4   h. 8

Pages 12 and 13
A. and, For example, and, Even more important, and
B. and, also, and
C. and, moreover, another, and, and, Besides, In addition, and
D. For instance, and, More than that

(Wording of answers may vary slightly.)
1. a telephone, some coins, recordings, a Bible, a novel, baseball cards, and a toothbrush (At least 3 should be mentioned.)
2. the story of our civilization and its achievements
3. placed in small safes in the cornerstones of buildings
4. a car with a full tank of gasoline
5. coins, stamps, trading cards, and toys

Pages 14 and 15
A. Apparently, clearly
B. Obviously, We can see, Apparently, As a result, In effect

(Wordings of answers may vary slightly.)
1. he repeated the error when he played it back
2. playing in concert halls all over America and Europe
3. was not even interested in music
4. we do not understand how his gift worked

Pages 16 and 17
A. ———
B. Despite, Nevertheless, however, Instead, Even though
C. in fact, although, anyhow

1. Despite   4. Even though
2. Nevertheless   5. in fact
3. however   6. Although

Pages 18 and 19
A. primarily, especially
B. principal
C. most important

(Wording of answers may vary slightly.)
1. to make fun of Americans
2. they thought they were better soldiers than the British
3. was "Yankee Doodle"
4. national song to come out of the Revolutionary War period

Pages 20 and 21
A. also
B. After
   principal
   In the beginning
   However
C. Even though
   but
   After
   In fact
   As a result
D. Despite

Pages 22 and 23
1. traveling   A. c
2. bad   B. b
3. return   C. c
4. goal
5. first

Pages 24 and 25
1. buildings   A. a
2. domes   B. c
3. controlled   C. c
4. covered   D. b
5. live

Pages 26 and 27
1. messages   A. b
2. enemy   B. a
3. pigeons   C. c
4. American   D. c
5. photographed
6. capsule

Pages 28 and 29
Problem: Time was needed to reach the king before the sentence could be carried out.
Solution: The messenger could not deliver the order for Sir John's death.
Steps: 1. Gizelle disguised herself as a masked highwayman. 2. Gizelle held up the messenger. 3. Gizelle stole the papers with the death sentence.
Proof: Sir John's life was saved.

Pages 30 and 31
(Wording of answers may vary slightly.)
Problem: living things come only from living things (or: nonliving things could not come to life)
Solution: did not come from rotten meat
Steps (in any order):
1. open at the top
2. tightly covered with a lid
3. covered with a piece of screening

Proof: was open at the top

Pages 32 and 33
(Wording of answers may vary slightly.)
Problem: their wings would develop thick layers of ice
Possible solutions that did not work:
1. change altitude (or: fly at a lower altitude)
2. were directed toward the wings
3. Electric heating wires

Solution: a de-icer—a flat rubber tube that can be inflated and deflated
Proof: Every airplane manufactured today has a de-icer.

Pages 34 and 35
I. Romana Bañuelos became a successful businesswoman.
   A. She started a tortilla stand.
   B. The tortilla stand grew into a large company.
II. Romana Bañuelos helped other Mexican-Americans.
   B. She started a college scholarship program.
III. (In any order)
   A. She signed all United States government checks.
   B. Her signature appeared on U.S. paper money.
   C. She supervised the destruction of worn-out money.
   D. She was the first Mexican-American Treasurer of the United States.

Pages 36 and 37
I. It is important to maintain the balance of the food chain.
   A. We do not know what effect our interference will have on future life.
   C. Some kinds of whales are in danger of becoming extinct.
II. There are selfish reasons for not killing whales.
   B. We may run short of protein from land animals and fish.
   C. Whales may be an important source of protein.
III. There are moral reasons for not killing whales.
   A. 1. Whales care for their young.
      2. Whales travel in families.
   B. 1. Whales can perform complex tricks.
      2. Whales sing songs and communicate with each other.

Pages 38 and 39
A. b   C. b
B. c   D. a

1. set many records
2. pilot a plane around the world
3. began to run out of fuel
4. radioed her probable position

Pages 40 and 41
(Wording of answers may vary slightly.)
1. burning itself up (A new phoenix would arise from the ashes.)
2. clean dirty water and make poisonous drinks harmless
3. it had the head and wings of an eagle joined to the body of a lion

Page 42
Main idea: b
Supporting details: (Answers may vary in wording and organization.)
1. The captain said, "Take her down, emergency!" and they are at sea.
2. A horn sounded and "Dive! Dive!" was heard.
3. The ship is trying to get below 500 feet to get out of range of an enemy ship's sound equipment.

Page 43
Main idea: c
Supporting details: (Answers may vary in wording and organization.)
1. Ellen says, "We must find help soon."
2. Steve asks, "Do you think anyone will find us?"
3. Ellen left a note in the car in case someone can go after them or send help.

Pages 44 and 45
Main idea: c
Supporting details: (Answers may vary in wording and organization.)
1. Margaret had always been helpful and dependable.
2. The grain and water were now gone, and the hole in the wall was a chance for Margaret to get out.
3. In the past, she had shared her food and water, so it was not likely that she would have gone to the enemy because she was hungry.
4. Before she left, Margaret had left bread and soup for the soldiers. If she had escaped to save herself or to go to the enemy, she probably would have eaten first and not worried about hungry soldiers.

Page 46
Main idea: c
Supporting details: (Answers may vary in wording.)
1. The rope on the life preserver is short, so she cannot throw.
2. The boat has no oars, so she cannot row.